~ All Time ~

FAMILY FAVORITES™

GRANDMA'S OLD-FASHIONED COOKIES

PUBLICATIONS INTERNATIONAL, LTD.

— Contents —

COOKIE-JAR FAVORITES

CHOCOLATE-DIPPED ALMOND HORNS

1½ **cups powdered sugar**
1 **cup butter or margarine, softened**
2 **egg yolks**
1½ **teaspoons vanilla**
2 **cups all-purpose flour**
½ **cup ground almonds**
1 **teaspoon cream of tartar**
1 **teaspoon baking soda**
1 **cup semisweet chocolate chips, melted**
Powdered sugar

Preheat oven to 325°F. In large bowl, combine powdered sugar and butter. Beat at medium speed until creamy. Add egg yolks and vanilla; continue beating until well blended. Reduce speed to low. Add flour, almonds, cream of tartar and baking soda. Continue beating until well mixed. Shape into 1-inch balls. Roll balls into 2-inch ropes; shape into crescents. Place 2 inches apart on cookie sheets. Flatten slightly with bottom of glass covered in waxed paper. Bake for 8 to 10 minutes or until set. (Cookies do not brown.) Cool completely. Dip half of each cookie into chocolate; sprinkle remaining half with powdered sugar. Refrigerate until set.

Makes about 3 dozen cookies

OATMEAL APPLE COOKIES

¾ **CRISCO® Stick or ¾ cup CRISCO®**
All-Vegetable Shortening
1¼ **cups firmly packed brown sugar**
 1 **egg**
¼ **cup milk**
1½ **teaspoons vanilla**
 1 **cup all-purpose flour**
1¼ **teaspoons ground cinnamon**
½ **teaspoon salt**
¼ **teaspoon baking soda**
¼ **teaspoon ground nutmeg**
 3 **cups quick oats (not instant or**
    old-fashioned)
 1 **cup peeled, diced apples**
¾ **cup raisins (optional)**
¾ **cup coarsely chopped walnuts (optional)**

1. Preheat oven to 375°F. Grease cookie sheet with shortening.

2. Combine shortening, sugar, egg, milk and vanilla in large bowl. Beat at medium speed of electric mixer until well blended.

3. Combine flour, cinnamon, salt, baking soda and nutmeg in small bowl. Mix into creamed mixture at low speed until just blended. Stir in, one at a time, oats, apples, raisins and nuts with spoon.

4. Drop rounded tablespoonfuls of dough 2 inches apart onto cookie sheet.

5. Bake at 375°F for 13 minutes or until set. Cool 2 minutes on cookie sheet. Remove to wire rack. Cool completely.   *Makes about 2½ dozen cookies*

PEANUT BUTTER SENSATIONS

½ **CRISCO® Stick or ½ cup CRISCO®**
All-Vegetable Shortening
 1 **cup JIF® Creamy Peanut Butter**
¾ **cup granulated sugar**
½ **cup firmly packed brown sugar**
 1 **tablespoon milk**
 1 **teaspoon vanilla**
 1 **egg**
1¼ **cups all-purpose flour**
¾ **teaspoon baking soda**
½ **teaspoon baking powder**
¼ **teaspoon salt**

1. Preheat oven to 375°F.

2. Combine shortening, peanut butter, granulated sugar, brown sugar, milk and vanilla in large bowl. Beat at medium speed of electric mixer until well blended. Beat in egg.

3. Combine flour, baking soda, baking powder and salt in small bowl. Mix into creamed mixture at low speed until just blended. Drop rounded tablespoonfuls of dough 2 inches apart onto ungreased cookie sheet. Make crisscross pattern on dough with floured fork.

4. Bake at 375°F for 8 to 10 minutes. Cool 2 minutes on cookie sheet. Remove to wire rack. Cool completely.   *Makes about 2 dozen cookies*

Oatmeal Apple Cookies

CHOCOLATE SUGAR COOKIES

3 squares BAKER'S® Unsweetened Chocolate
1 cup (2 sticks) margarine or butter
1 cup sugar
1 egg
1 teaspoon vanilla
2 cups all-purpose flour
1 teaspoon baking soda
¼ teaspoon salt
Additional sugar

MICROWAVE chocolate and margarine in large microwavable bowl on HIGH 2 minutes or until margarine is melted. **Stir until chocolate is completely melted.**

STIR 1 cup sugar into melted chocolate mixture until well blended. Stir in egg and vanilla until completely mixed. Mix in flour, baking soda and salt. Refrigerate 30 minutes.

HEAT oven to 375°F. Shape dough into 1-inch balls; roll in additional sugar. Place on ungreased cookie sheets. (If a flatter, crisper cookie is desired, flatten ball with bottom of drinking glass.)

BAKE for 8 to 10 minutes or until set. Remove from cookie sheets to cool on wire racks.
Makes about 3½ dozen cookies

Prep Time: 15 minutes
Chill Time: 30 minutes
Baking Time: 8 to 10 minutes

JAM-FILLED CHOCOLATE SUGAR COOKIES: PREPARE Chocolate Sugar Cookie dough as directed. Roll in finely chopped nuts in place of sugar. Make indentation in each ball; fill center with your favorite jam. Bake as directed.

CHOCOLATE-CARAMEL SUGAR COOKIES: PREPARE Chocolate Sugar Cookie dough as directed. Roll in finely chopped nuts in place of sugar. Make indentation in each ball; bake as directed. Microwave 1 package (14 ounces) KRAFT® Caramels with 2 tablespoons milk in microwavable bowl on HIGH 3 minutes or until melted, stirring after 2 minutes. Fill centers of cookies with caramel mixture. Drizzle with melted BAKER'S® Semi-Sweet Chocolate.

Top to bottom: Chocolate Sugar Cookies, Jam-Filled Chocolate Sugar Cookies, Chocolate-Caramel Sugar Cookies

JAM-UP OATMEAL COOKIES

**1 CRISCO® Stick or 1 cup CRISCO®
All-Vegetable Shortening
1½ cups firmly packed brown sugar
2 eggs
2 teaspoons almond extract
2 cups all-purpose flour
1 teaspoon baking powder
1 teaspoon salt
½ teaspoon baking soda
2½ cups quick oats (not instant or
old-fashioned), uncooked
1 cup finely chopped pecans
1 jar (12 ounces) strawberry jam
Sugar for sprinkling**

1. Combine shortening and brown sugar in large bowl. Beat at medium speed of electric mixer until well blended. Beat in eggs and almond extract.

2. Combine flour, baking powder, salt and baking soda in small bowl. Mix into creamed mixture at low speed until just blended. Stir in oats and chopped nuts with spoon. Cover and refrigerate at least 1 hour.

3. Preheat oven to 350°F. Grease cookie sheet with shortening. Roll out dough, half at a time, to about ¼-inch thickness on floured surface. Cut out with 2½-inch round cookie cutter. Place 1 teaspoonful of jam in center of half of the rounds. Top with remaining rounds. Press edges to seal. Prick centers; sprinkle with sugar. Place 1 inch apart on cookie sheet.

4. Bake 12 to 15 minutes or until lightly browned. Cool 2 minutes on cookie sheet. Remove to wire rack. Cool completely.

Makes about 2 dozen cookies

PEANUT BUTTER JEWELS

**1 package DUNCAN HINES® Peanut Butter
Cookie Mix
1 egg
¼ cup CRISCO® Oil
1 tablespoon water
⅓ cup sugar
⅓ cup cocktail peanuts, finely chopped
Strawberry jam
Apricot preserves**

1. Preheat oven to 375°F.

2. Combine cookie mix, peanut butter flavor packet from Mix, egg, oil and water in large bowl. Stir until thoroughly blended. Shape dough into 48 (1-inch) balls. Roll half the balls in sugar and half in chopped peanuts. Place 2 inches apart on ungreased cookie sheets. Make indentation in center of each ball with finger or handle end of wooden spoon. Fill with ¼ teaspoon strawberry jam or apricot preserves. Bake at 375°F for 8 to 10 minutes or until light golden brown. Cool 1 minute on cookie sheets. Remove to wire racks. Cool completely. Store in airtight containers.

Makes 4 dozen cookies

TIP: For a delicious flavor variation, try seedless red raspberry or blackberry jam.

Jam-Up Oatmeal Cookies

CINNAMON-APRICOT TART OATMEAL COOKIES

- ½ **cup water**
- 1 **package (8 ounces) dried apricot halves, diced**
- 1 **CRISCO® Stick or 1 cup CRISCO® All-Vegetable Shortening**
- 1 **cup firmly packed brown sugar**
- ¼ **cup granulated sugar**
- 1 **egg**
- 2 **teaspoons vanilla**
- 1½ **cups all-purpose flour**
- 2 **teaspoons ground cinnamon**
- 1 **teaspoon baking soda**
- 1 **teaspoon salt**
- 1 **cup plus 2 tablespoons chopped pecans**
- 3 **cups quick oats (not instant or old-fashioned)**

1. Place ½ cup water in small saucepan. Heat to boiling. Place diced apricots in strainer over boiling water. Reduce heat to low. Cover. Steam for 15 minutes. Cool. Reserve liquid.

2. Preheat oven to 375°F. Grease cookie sheet. Combine shortening, brown sugar, granulated sugar, egg and vanilla in large bowl. Beat at medium speed of electric mixer until well blended.

3. Combine flour, cinnamon, baking soda and salt in small bowl. Mix into creamed mixture at low speed until just blended. Stir in nuts, apricots and reserved liquid from apricots. Stir in oats with spoon. Drop rounded tablespoonfuls of dough 2 inches apart onto cookie sheet.

4. Bake at 375°F for 10 to 11 minutes. Cool 2 minutes on cookie sheet. Remove to wire rack. Cool completely. *Makes 3½ to 4 dozen cookies*

EASY LEMON COOKIES

- 1 **package DUNCAN HINES® Moist Deluxe Lemon Cake Mix**
- 2 **eggs**
- ½ **cup CRISCO® Oil**
- 1 **teaspoon grated lemon peel**
  Pecan halves, for garnish

1. Preheat oven to 350°F.

2. Combine cake mix, eggs, oil and lemon peel in large bowl. Stir until thoroughly blended. Drop by rounded teaspoonfuls 2 inches apart onto ungreased cookie sheets. Press pecan half in center of each cookie. Bake at 350°F for 9 to 11 minutes or until edges are light golden brown. Cool 1 minute on cookie sheets. Remove to wire racks. Cool completely. Store in airtight container.

Makes 4 dozen cookies

TIP: You may substitute whole almonds or walnut halves for the pecan halves.

Top to bottom: Chocolate-Orange Chip Cookies (page 48), Cinnamon-Apricot Tart Oatmeal Cookies

KENTUCKY BOURBON PECAN TARTS

Cream Cheese Pastry (recipe follows)
2 eggs
½ cup granulated sugar
½ cup KARO® Light or Dark Corn Syrup
2 tablespoons bourbon
1 tablespoon MAZOLA® Margarine, melted
½ teaspoon vanilla
1 cup chopped pecans
Powdered sugar (optional)

Preheat oven to 350°F. Prepare Cream Cheese Pastry. Divide dough in half; set aside one half. On floured surface, roll out pastry to ⅛-inch thickness. *If necessary, add small amount of flour to keep pastry from sticking.* Cut into 12 (2¼-inch) rounds. Press evenly into bottoms and up sides of 1¾-inch muffin pan cups. Repeat with remaining pastry. Refrigerate.

In medium bowl, beat eggs slightly. Stir in granulated sugar, corn syrup, bourbon, margarine and vanilla until well blended. Spoon 1 heaping teaspoon pecans into each pastry-lined cup; top with 1 tablespoon corn syrup mixture.

Bake 20 to 25 minutes or until lightly browned and toothpick inserted into center comes out clean. Cool in pans 5 minutes. Remove; cool completely on wire rack. If desired, sprinkle cookies with powdered sugar.

Makes about 2 dozen cookies

CREAM CHEESE PASTRY

1 cup all-purpose flour
¾ teaspoon baking powder
Pinch salt
½ cup MAZOLA® Margarine, softened
1 package (3 ounces) cream cheese, softened
2 teaspoons sugar

In small bowl, combine flour, baking powder and salt. In large bowl, mix margarine, cream cheese and sugar until well combined. Stir in flour mixture until well blended. Press firmly into ball with hands.

Prep Time: 45 minutes
Bake Time: 25 minutes, plus cooling

Top to bottom: Brandy Lace Cookies (page 30), Kentucky Bourbon Pecan Tarts

AUSTRIAN TEA COOKIES

1½ **cups sugar, divided**
½ **cup butter, softened**
½ **cup vegetable shortening**
 1 **egg, beaten**
½ **teaspoon vanilla extract**
 2 **cups all-purpose flour**
 2 **cups ALMOND DELIGHT® Brand Cereal,
    crushed to 1 cup**
½ **teaspoon baking powder**
¼ **teaspoon ground cinnamon**
 14 **ounces almond paste**
 2 **egg whites**
 5 **tablespoons raspberry or apricot jam,
    warmed**

In large bowl, beat 1 cup sugar, butter and
shortening. Add egg and vanilla; mix well. Stir in
flour, cereal, baking powder and cinnamon until
well blended. Refrigerate 1 to 2 hours or until
firm.

Preheat oven to 350°F. Roll dough out on lightly
floured surface to ¼-inch thickness; cut into
2-inch circles with floured cookie cutter. Place on
ungreased cookie sheet; set aside. In small bowl,
beat almond paste, egg whites and remaining ½
cup sugar until smooth. With pastry tube fitted
with medium-sized star tip, pipe almond paste
mixture ½ inch thick on top of each cookie along
outside edge. Place ¼ teaspoon jam in center of
each cookie, spreading out to paste. Bake 8 to 10
minutes or until lightly browned. Let stand 1
minute before removing from cookie sheet. Cool
on wire rack.   *Makes about 3½ dozen cookies*

BRANDY LACE COOKIES

¼ **cup sugar**
¼ **cup MAZOLA® Margarine**
¼ **cup KARO® Light or Dark Corn Syrup**
½ **cup all-purpose flour**
¼ **cup very finely chopped pecans or
    walnuts**
 2 **tablespoons brandy**
    **Melted white and/or semisweet chocolate
    (optional)**

Preheat oven to 350°F. Lightly grease and flour
cookie sheets.

In small saucepan, combine sugar, margarine and
corn syrup. Bring to boil over medium heat,
stirring constantly. Remove from heat. Stir in flour,
pecans and brandy. Drop 12 evenly spaced half
teaspoonfuls of batter onto prepared cookie sheets.

Bake 6 minutes or until golden. Cool 1 to 2
minutes or until cookies can be lifted but are still
warm and pliable; remove with spatula. Curl
around handle of wooden spoon; slide off when
crisp. If cookies harden before curling, return to
oven to soften. If desired, drizzle with melted
chocolate.   *Makes 4 to 5 dozen cookies*

Prep Time: 30 minutes
Bake Time: 6 minutes, plus curling and cooling

Austrian Tea Cookies

COOKIE-JAR FAVORITES

PEANUT BUTTER SECRETS

COOKIES
1 CRISCO® Stick or 1 cup CRISCO®
    All-Vegetable Shortening
¾ cup firmly packed brown sugar
½ cup granulated sugar
½ cup JIF® Creamy Peanut Butter
1 egg
1 teaspoon vanilla
2 cups all-purpose flour
1 teaspoon baking soda
½ teaspoon salt
40 to 45 chocolate-covered miniature peanut
    butter cups, unwrapped

GLAZE
1 teaspoon CRISCO® All-Vegetable
    Shortening
1 cup semi-sweet chocolate chips
2 tablespoons JIF® Creamy Peanut Butter

1. Preheat oven to 375°F. Grease cookie sheet with shortening.

2. For Cookies, combine shortening, brown sugar, granulated sugar and peanut butter in large bowl. Beat at medium speed of electric mixer until well blended. Beat in egg and vanilla.

3. Combine flour, baking soda and salt in small bowl. Mix into creamed mixture at low speed until just blended.

4. Form rounded teaspoonfuls of dough around each peanut butter cup. Enclose entirely. Place 2 inches apart on cookie sheet.

5. Bake 8 to 10 minutes or until cookies are just browned. Remove immediately to wire rack.

6. For Glaze, combine shortening, chocolate chips and peanut butter in microwave-safe cup. Microwave at 50% (MEDIUM). Stir after 1 minute. Repeat until smooth (or melt on rangetop in small saucepan on very low heat). Dip cookie tops in glaze.   *Makes about 3½ dozen cookies*

QUICK CHOCOLATE MACAROONS

1 square BAKER'S® Unsweetened
    Chocolate
1⅓ cups BAKER'S® ANGEL FLAKE® Coconut
⅓ cup sweetened condensed milk
½ teaspoon vanilla

HEAT oven to 350°F.

MELT chocolate in large microwavable bowl on HIGH 1 to 2 minutes or until almost melted, stirring after each minute. **Stir until chocolate is completely melted.** Stir in coconut, condensed milk and vanilla. Drop from teaspoonfuls, 1 inch apart, onto well greased cookie sheets.

BAKE for 10 to 12 minutes or until set. Immediately remove from cookie sheets to cool on wire racks.   *Makes about 2 dozen cookies*

Prep Time: 10 minutes
Baking Time: 10 to 12 minutes

Peanut Butter Secrets

CHIPS & CHUNKS

PEANUT BUTTER CHOCOLATE CHIPPERS

1 cup creamy or chunky peanut butter
1 cup firmly packed light brown sugar
1 large egg
¾ cup milk chocolate chips
Granulated sugar

1. Preheat oven to 350°F.

2. Combine peanut butter, brown sugar and egg in medium bowl with mixing spoon until well blended. Add chips; mix well.

3. Roll heaping tablespoonfuls of dough into 1½-inch balls. Place balls 2 inches apart on *ungreased* cookie sheets.

4. Dip table fork into granulated sugar; press criss-cross fashion onto each ball, flattening to ½-inch thickness.

5. Bake 12 minutes or until set. Let cookies stand on cookie sheets 2 minutes. Remove cookies with spatula to wire racks; cool completely. Store tightly covered at room temperature or freeze up to 3 months.   *Makes about 2 dozen cookies*

CHIPS & CHUNKS

OATMEAL CANDIED CHIPPERS

¾ **cup all-purpose flour**
¾ **teaspoon salt**
½ **teaspoon baking soda**
¾ **cup butter or margarine, softened**
¾ **cup granulated sugar**
¾ **cup firmly packed light brown sugar**
3 **tablespoons milk**
1 **large egg**
2 **teaspoons vanilla**
3 **cups uncooked quick-cooking or old-fashioned oats**
1⅓ **cups (10-ounce package) candy-coated semisweet chocolate chips***

*Or, substitute 1 cup (8-ounce package) candy-coated milk chocolate chips.

1. Preheat oven to 375°F. Grease cookie sheets; set aside.

2. Combine flour, salt and baking soda in small bowl.

3. Beat butter, granulated sugar and brown sugar in large bowl with electric mixer at medium speed until light and fluffy. Add milk, egg and vanilla; beat well. Add flour mixture. Beat at low speed until blended. Stir in oats and chips.

4. Drop dough by tablespoonfuls 2 inches apart onto prepared cookie sheets.**

**Or, use a small ice cream scoop (#80) filled with dough and pressed against side of bowl to level.

5. Bake 10 to 11 minutes or until edges are golden brown. Let cookies stand 2 minutes on cookie sheets. Remove cookies with spatula to wire racks; cool completely. Store tightly covered at room temperature or freeze up to 3 months.

Makes about 4 dozen cookies

CHOCOLATE-PEANUT COOKIES

1 **cup butter or margarine, softened**
¾ **cup granulated sugar**
¾ **cup firmly packed light brown sugar**
2 **eggs**
1 **teaspoon vanilla**
1 **teaspoon baking soda**
¼ **teaspoon salt**
2¼ **cups all-purpose flour**
2 **cups chocolate-covered peanuts**

Preheat oven to 375°F. Line cookie sheets with parchment paper or leave ungreased. Beat butter, granulated sugar, brown sugar, eggs and vanilla in large bowl with electric mixer until fluffy. Beat in baking soda and salt. Stir in flour to make stiff dough. Blend in chocolate-covered peanuts. Drop by rounded teaspoonfuls 2 inches apart onto cookie sheets. Bake 9 to 11 minutes or until just barely golden. *Do not overbake.* Remove to wire racks to cool. *Makes about 5 dozen cookies*

Oatmeal Candied Chippers

CHIPS & CHUNKS

CHOCOLATE CHIP SANDWICH COOKIES

COOKIES
   1 package DUNCAN HINES® Chocolate Chip
      Cookie Mix
   1 egg
   ⅓ cup CRISCO® Oil
   3 tablespoons water

CREAM FILLING
   1½ cups marshmallow creme
    ¾ cup butter or margarine, softened
   2½ cups powdered sugar
   1½ teaspoons vanilla extract

1. Preheat oven to 375°F.

2. For Cookies, combine cookie mix, egg, oil and water in large bowl. Stir until thoroughly blended. Drop by rounded teaspoonfuls 2 inches apart onto ungreased cookie sheets. Bake at 375°F for 8 to 10 minutes or until light golden brown. Cool 1 minute on cookie sheets. Remove to wire racks.

3. For Cream Filling, combine marshmallow creme and butter in large bowl. Add powdered sugar and vanilla extract, beating until smooth.

4. To assemble, spread bottoms of half the cookies with 1 tablespoon cream filling; top with remaining cookies. Press together to make sandwich cookies. Refrigerate to quickly firm the filling, if desired.

Makes about 24 sandwich cookies

TIP: After chilling the assembled cookies, wrap individually in plastic wrap. Store in the refrigerator until ready to serve.

QUICK CHOCOLATE SOFTIES

   1 package (18.25 ounces) devil's food
      chocolate cake mix
   ⅓ cup water
   ¼ cup butter or margarine, softened
   1 large egg
   1 cup large vanilla baking chips
   ½ cup coarsely chopped walnuts

1. Preheat oven to 350°F. Lightly grease cookie sheets.

2. Combine cake mix, water, butter and egg in large bowl. Beat with electric mixer at low speed until moistened. Increase speed to medium; beat 1 minute. (Dough will be thick.) Stir in chips and walnuts with mixing spoon until well blended.

3. Drop heaping *teaspoonfuls* of dough 2 inches apart (for smaller cookies) or heaping *tablespoonfuls* of dough 3 inches apart (for larger cookies) onto prepared cookie sheets.

4. Bake 10 to 12 minutes or until set. Let cookies stand on cookie sheets 1 minute. Remove cookies with spatula to wire racks; cool completely. Store tightly covered at room temperature or freeze up to 3 months.

Makes about 2 dozen large or 4 dozen small cookies

Chocolate Chip Sandwich Cookies

OATMEAL SCOTCHIES

1¼ cups all-purpose flour
1 teaspoon baking soda
½ teaspoon salt
½ teaspoon ground cinnamon
1 cup (2 sticks) butter or margarine, softened
¾ cup granulated sugar
¾ cup packed brown sugar
2 eggs
1 teaspoon vanilla extract or grated peel of 1 orange
3 cups quick *or* old-fashioned oats
2 cups (12-ounce package) NESTLÉ® TOLL HOUSE® Butterscotch Flavored Morsels

COMBINE flour, baking soda, salt and cinnamon in small bowl. Beat butter, granulated sugar, brown sugar, eggs and vanilla in large mixing bowl until creamy. Gradually beat in flour mixture. Stir in oats and morsels. Drop by rounded tablespoons onto ungreased cookie sheets.

BAKE in preheated 375°F oven for 7 to 8 minutes for chewy cookies, 9 to 10 minutes for crisp cookies. Let stand for 2 minutes; remove to wire racks to cool completely.   *Makes 4 dozen cookies*

CHOCO-SCUTTERBOTCH

⅔ CRISCO® Stick or ⅔ cup CRISCO® All-Vegetable Shortening
½ cup firmly packed brown sugar
2 eggs
1 package DUNCAN HINES® Moist Deluxe Yellow Cake Mix
1 cup toasted rice cereal
½ cup milk chocolate chunks
½ cup butterscotch chips
½ cup semi-sweet chocolate chips
½ cup coarsely chopped walnuts or pecans

1. Preheat oven to 375°F.

2. Combine shortening and brown sugar in large bowl. Beat at medium speed of electric mixer until well blended. Beat in eggs.

3. Add cake mix gradually at low speed. Mix until well blended. Stir in cereal, chocolate chunks, butterscotch chips, chocolate chips and nuts with spoon until well blended. Shape dough into 1¼-inch balls. Place 2 inches apart on ungreased cookie sheet. Flatten slightly. Shape sides to form circle, if necessary.

4. Bake at 375°F for 7 to 9 minutes or until lightly browned around edges. Cool 2 minutes before removing to paper towels to cool completely.
Makes about 3 dozen cookies

Oatmeal Scotchies

— *Keepsake* —

BAR COOKIES

CHOCOLATE CHIP SHORTBREAD

- ½ **cup butter, softened**
- ½ **cup sugar**
- 1 **teaspoon vanilla**
- 1 **cup all-purpose flour**
- ¼ **teaspoon salt**
- ½ **cup mini semisweet chocolate chips**

Preheat oven to 375°F. Beat butter and sugar in large bowl with electric mixer at medium speed until light and fluffy. Beat in vanilla. Add flour and salt. Stir in chips.

Divide dough in half. Press each half into ungreased 8-inch round cake pan. Bake 12 minutes or until edges are golden brown. Score shortbread with sharp knife, taking care not to cut completely through shortbread. Make 8 wedges per pan.

Let pans stand on wire racks 10 minutes. Invert shortbread onto wire racks; cool completely. Break into wedges.   *Makes 16 cookies*

BAR COOKIES

PEANUT BUTTER BARS

½ **CRISCO® Stick or ½ cup CRISCO®**
   All-Vegetable Shortening
1½ **cups firmly packed brown sugar**
⅔ **cup JIF® Creamy or Extra Crunchy Peanut**
   Butter
2 **eggs**
1 **teaspoon vanilla**
1½ **cups all-purpose flour**
½ **teaspoon salt**
¼ **cup milk**

1. Preheat oven to 350°F. Grease 13×9×2-inch baking pan.

2. Combine shortening, brown sugar and peanut butter in large bowl. Beat at medium speed of electric mixer until well blended. Beat in eggs and vanilla.

3. Combine flour and salt in small bowl. Add alternately with milk to creamed mixture at low speed. Beat until well blended. Spread in pan.

4. Bake 28 to 32 minutes or until golden brown and center is set. Cool in pan on wire rack. Top with frosting or glaze, if desired. Cut into 2¼×1½-inch bars.   *Makes 32 bars*

Frosting and Glaze Variations

CHOCOLATE DREAM FROSTING:

Combine 2 tablespoons CRISCO® All-Vegetable Shortening, 1 cup miniature marshmallows, 1 square (1 ounce) unsweetened chocolate and 3 tablespoons milk in medium microwave-safe bowl. Cover with waxed paper. Microwave at 50% (MEDIUM). Stir after 1 minute. Repeat until smooth (or melt on rangetop in medium saucepan on low heat). Stir in 1¾ cups powdered sugar. Beat until well blended. Spread over top. Sprinkle ¼ cup finely chopped peanuts over frosting. Set aside until frosting is firm. Cut into bars.

MICROWAVE CHOCOLATE CHIP GLAZE:

Combine 1 tablespoon CRISCO® All-Vegetable Shortening, ¼ cup semi-sweet chocolate chips and 3 tablespoons milk in medium microwave-safe bowl. Microwave at 50% (MEDIUM). Stir after 1 minute. Repeat until smooth (or melt on rangetop in small saucepan on very low heat). Add ½ cup powdered sugar and ¼ teaspoon vanilla. Stir until smooth. (Add small amount of hot milk if thinner consistency is desired.) Drizzle over top. Sprinkle ¼ cup finely chopped peanuts over glaze. Set aside until glaze is firm. Cut into bars.

Top to bottom: "Cordially Yours" Chocolate Chip Bars (page 56), Peanut Butter Bars

BAR COOKIES

CALIFORNIA APRICOT POWER BARS

2 cups California dried apricot halves,
  coarsely chopped (12 ounces)
2½ cups pecans, coarsely chopped
  (10 ounces)
1¼ cups pitted dates, coarsely chopped
  (8 ounces)
1¼ cups whole wheat flour
1 teaspoon baking powder
1 cup firmly packed brown sugar
3 large eggs
¼ cup apple juice or water
1½ teaspoons vanilla

Preheat oven to 350°F. Line 15½×10½×1-inch jelly-roll pan with foil. In large bowl, stir together apricots, pecans and dates; divide in half. In small bowl, combine flour and baking powder; add to half of fruit-nut mixture. Toss to coat. In medium bowl, combine brown sugar, eggs, apple juice and vanilla; stir into flour mixture until thoroughly moistened. Spread batter evenly into prepared pan. Lightly press remaining fruit-nut mixture on top.

Bake 20 minutes or until bars are golden and spring back when pressed lightly. Cool in pan 5 minutes. Turn out onto wire rack; cool 45 minutes. Peel off foil and cut into bars. Store in airtight container. Bars may be frozen.

Makes about 32 bars

Favorite recipe from **California Apricot Advisory Board**

"CORDIALLY YOURS" CHOCOLATE CHIP BARS

¾ CRISCO® Stick or ¾ cup CRISCO®
  All-Vegetable Shortening
2 eggs
½ cup granulated sugar
¼ cup firmly packed brown sugar
1½ teaspoons vanilla
1 teaspoon almond extract
2 cups all-purpose flour
1 teaspoon baking soda
½ teaspoon ground cinnamon
1 can (21 ounces) cherry pie filling
1½ cups milk chocolate big chips
  Powdered sugar

1. Preheat oven to 350°F. Grease 15½×10½×1-inch jelly-roll pan.

2. Combine shortening, eggs, granulated sugar, brown sugar, vanilla and almond extract in large bowl. Beat at medium speed of electric mixer until well blended.

3. Combine flour, baking soda and cinnamon in medium bowl. Mix into creamed mixture at low speed until just blended. Stir in pie filling and chocolate chips. Spread in pan.

4. Bake 25 minutes or until lightly browned and top springs back when lightly pressed. Cool completely in pan on wire rack. Sprinkle with powdered sugar. Cut into 2½×2-inch bars.

Makes 30 bars

California Apricot Power Bars

BAR COOKIES

LAYERED CHOCOLATE CHEESE BARS

¼ **cup (½ stick) margarine or butter**
1½ **cups graham cracker crumbs**
¾ **cup sugar**
1 **package (4 ounces) BAKER'S®**
    GERMAN'S® Sweet Chocolate, melted
1 **package (8 ounces) PHILADELPHIA**
    BRAND® Cream Cheese, softened
1 **egg**
1 **cup BAKER'S® ANGEL FLAKE® Coconut**
1 **cup chopped nuts**

HEAT oven to 350°F.

MELT margarine in oven in 13×9-inch pan. Add graham cracker crumbs and ¼ cup of the sugar; mix well. Press into pan. Bake for 10 minutes.

COMBINE melted chocolate, the remaining ½ cup sugar, the cream cheese and egg. Spread over crust. Sprinkle with coconut and nuts; press lightly.

BAKE for 30 minutes. Cool; cut into bars.

Makes about 24 bars

Prep Time: 20 minutes
Baking Time: 40 minutes

BANANA SPLIT BARS

⅓ **cup margarine or butter, softened**
1 **cup sugar**
1 **egg**
1 **banana, mashed**
½ **teaspoon vanilla**
1¼ **cups all-purpose flour**
1 **teaspoon CALUMET® Baking Powder**
¼ **teaspoon salt**
⅓ **cup chopped nuts**
2 **cups KRAFT® Miniature Marshmallows**
1 **cup BAKER'S® Semi-Sweet Real**
    Chocolate Chips
⅓ **cup maraschino cherries, drained and**
    quartered

HEAT oven to 350°F.

BEAT margarine and sugar until light and fluffy. Add egg, banana and vanilla; mix well. Mix in flour, baking powder and salt. Stir in nuts. Pour into greased 13×9-inch pan.

BAKE for 20 minutes. Remove from oven. Sprinkle with marshmallows, chips and cherries. Bake 10 to 15 minutes longer or until toothpick inserted in center comes out clean. Cool in pan; cut into bars.   *Makes about 24 bars*

Prep Time: 20 minutes
Baking Time: 30 to 35 minutes

Top plate (clockwise from top): Layered Chocolate Cheese Bar,
Banana Split Bar, Chocolate Peanut Butter Bar (page 68)

BAR COOKIES

PEACHY OATMEAL BARS

CRUMB MIXTURE
1½ cups all-purpose flour
1 cup uncooked rolled oats
¾ cup margarine, melted
½ cup sugar
2 teaspoons almond extract
½ teaspoon baking soda
¼ teaspoon salt

FILLING
¾ cup peach or apricot preserves
⅓ cup flaked coconut

Preheat oven to 350°F.

For Crumb Mixture, combine all crumb mixture ingredients in large bowl of electric mixer. Beat at low speed, scraping bowl often, until mixture is crumbly, 1 to 2 minutes. *Reserve ¾ cup crumb mixture;* press remaining crumb mixture onto bottom of greased 9-inch square baking pan.

For Filling, spread preserves to within ½ inch of edge of crust; sprinkle with reserved crumb mixture and coconut. Bake for 20 to 25 minutes or until edges are lightly browned. Cool completely. Cut into bars. *Makes about 24 bars*

STREUSEL STRAWBERRY BARS

1 cup butter or margarine, softened
1 cup sugar
2 cups all-purpose flour
1 egg
¾ cup pecans, coarsely chopped
1 jar (10 ounces) strawberry or raspberry preserves

Preheat oven to 350°F. Combine butter and sugar in large mixing bowl. Beat at low speed, scraping bowl often, until well blended. Add flour and egg. Beat until mixture is crumbly, 2 to 3 minutes. Stir in pecans. Reserve 1 cup crumb mixture; press remaining crumb mixture onto bottom of greased 9-inch square baking pan. Spread preserves to within ½ inch of edge of crust. Crumble reserved crumb mixture over preserves. Bake for 40 to 50 minutes or until lightly browned. Cool completely. Cut into bars. *Makes about 24 bars*

Top to bottom: Peachy Oatmeal Bars, Streusel Strawberry Bars

BAR COOKIES

CHUNKY MACADAMIA BARS

¾ cup (1½ sticks) butter or margarine, softened
1 cup firmly packed light brown sugar
½ cup granulated sugar
1 egg
1 teaspoon vanilla extract
2¼ cups all-purpose flour
1 teaspoon baking soda
¾ cup coarsely chopped macadamia nuts
1¾ cups (10-ounce package) HERSHEY®S Semi-Sweet Chocolate Chunks, divided
Quick Vanilla Glaze (recipe follows)

Preheat oven to 375°F. In large mixing bowl, beat butter, brown sugar and granulated sugar until creamy. Add egg and vanilla; beat well. Add flour and baking soda; blend well. Stir in nuts and 1 cup chocolate chunks. Press dough onto bottom of ungreased 13×9×2-inch baking pan. Sprinkle with remaining ¾ cup chocolate chunks. Bake 22 to 25 minutes or until golden brown. Cool completely in pan on wire rack. Prepare Quick Vanilla Glaze; drizzle over top of bars. Allow glaze to set. Cut into bars.   *Makes about 24 bars*

QUICK VANILLA GLAZE
1 cup powdered sugar
2 tablespoons milk
½ teaspoon vanilla extract

In small bowl, combine powdered sugar, milk and vanilla; stir until smooth and of desired consistency.

CHOCOLATE AMARETTO SQUARES

½ cup (1 stick) butter (do *not* use margarine), melted
1 cup sugar
2 eggs
½ cup all-purpose flour
⅓ cup HERSHEY®S Cocoa or HERSHEY®S European Style Cocoa
2 tablespoons almond flavored liqueur *or* ½ teaspoon almond extract
1¼ cups ground almonds
Sliced almonds (optional)

Preheat oven to 325°F. Grease 8-inch square baking pan. In large bowl, beat butter and sugar until creamy. Add eggs, flour and cocoa; beat well. Stir in almond liqueur and ground almonds. Pour batter into prepared pan. Bake 35 to 40 minutes or just until set. Cool completely in pan on wire rack. Cut into squares. Garnish with sliced almonds, if desired.   *Makes about 16 squares*

Clockwise from top: Chunky Macadamia Bars, Chocolate Amaretto Squares, Chocolate Pecan Pie Bars (page 64)

BAR COOKIES

HEATH® BARS

1 cup butter, softened
1 cup firmly packed brown sugar
1 egg yolk
1 teaspoon vanilla
2 cups all-purpose flour
18 to 19 Original HEATH® English Toffee
    Snack Size Bars, crushed, divided
½ cup finely chopped pecans

Preheat oven to 350°F. In large bowl, with electric mixer, beat butter well; blend in brown sugar, egg yolk and vanilla. By hand, mix in flour, ⅔ cup Heath® Bars and nuts. Press into ungreased 15½×10½-inch jelly-roll pan.

Bake 18 to 20 minutes or until browned. Remove from oven and immediately sprinkle remaining Heath® Bars over top. Cool slightly; cut into bars while warm. *Makes about 48 bars*

CHOCOLATE PEANUT BUTTER BARS

2 cups peanut butter
1 cup sugar
2 eggs
1 package (8 ounces) BAKER'S®
    Semi-Sweet Chocolate
1 cup chopped peanuts

HEAT oven to 350°F.

BEAT peanut butter, sugar and eggs in large bowl until light and fluffy. Reserve 1 cup peanut butter mixture; set aside.

MELT four squares of the chocolate. Add to peanut butter mixture in bowl; mix well. Press into ungreased 13×9-inch pan. Top with reserved peanut butter mixture.

BAKE for 30 minutes or until edges are lightly browned. Melt the remaining 4 squares chocolate; spread evenly over entire surface. Sprinkle with peanuts. Cool in pan until chocolate is set. Cut into bars. *Makes about 24 bars*

Prep Time: 15 minutes
Baking Time: 30 minutes

Heath® Bars

BAR COOKIES

LUSCIOUS LEMON BARS

CRUST
  ½ **cup butter or margarine, softened**
  ½ **cup granulated sugar**
    Grated peel of ½ SUNKIST® Lemon
  1¼ **cups all-purpose flour**

LEMON LAYER
  4 **eggs**
  1⅔ **cups granulated sugar**
  3 **tablespoons all-purpose flour**
  ½ **teaspoon baking powder**
    Grated peel of ½ SUNKIST® Lemon
    Juice of 2 SUNKIST® Lemons
      (6 tablespoons)
  1 **teaspoon vanilla extract**
    Powdered sugar

For Crust, in medium bowl, cream together butter, granulated sugar and lemon peel. Gradually stir in flour to form a soft crumbly dough. Press evenly into bottom of aluminum foil-lined 13×9×2-inch baking pan. Bake at 350° for 15 minutes.

For Lemon Layer, while crust is baking, in large bowl, whisk or beat eggs well. Stir together granulated sugar, flour and baking powder. Gradually whisk sugar mixture into eggs. Whisk in lemon peel, juice and vanilla. Pour over hot crust. Return to oven. Bake for 20 to 25 minutes or until top is lightly browned. Cool. Using foil on two sides, lift out cookie base. Gently loosen foil along all sides. With long wet knife, cut into bars or squares. Sprinkle tops with powdered sugar.

Makes about 3 dozen bars

BLUEBERRY CHEESECAKE BARS

  1 **package DUNCAN HINES® Blueberry**
    Muffin Mix
  ¼ **cup butter or margarine, softened**
  ⅓ **cup finely chopped pecans**
  1 **package (8 ounces) cream cheese,**
    softened
  ½ **cup sugar**
  1 **egg**
  3 **tablespoons lemon juice**
  1 **teaspoon grated lemon peel**

1. Preheat oven to 350°F. Grease 9-inch square baking pan.

2. Rinse blueberries from Mix with cold water and drain.

3. Place muffin mix in medium bowl. Cut in butter with pastry blender or two knives. Stir in pecans. Press into bottom of pan. Bake at 350°F for 15 minutes or until set.

4. Combine cream cheese and sugar in medium bowl. Beat until smooth. Add egg, lemon juice and lemon peel. Beat well. Spread over baked crust. Sprinkle with blueberries. Sprinkle topping packet from Mix over blueberries. Return to oven. Bake at 350°F for 35 to 40 minutes or until filling is set. Cool completely. Refrigerate until ready to serve. Cut into bars.   *Makes 16 bars*

Blueberry Cheesecake Bars

BAR COOKIES

TRIPLE LAYER PEANUT BUTTER BARS

BASE
1¼ cups firmly packed light brown sugar
¾ cup creamy peanut butter
½ CRISCO® Stick or ½ cup CRISCO® All-Vegetable Shortening
3 tablespoons milk
1 tablespoon vanilla
1 egg
1¾ cups all-purpose flour
¾ teaspoon baking soda
¾ teaspoon salt

PEANUT BUTTER LAYER
1½ cups powdered sugar
2 tablespoons creamy peanut butter
1 tablespoon CRISCO® All-Vegetable Shortening
3 tablespoons milk

CHOCOLATE GLAZE
2 squares (1 ounce each) unsweetened baking chocolate
2 tablespoons CRISCO® All-Vegetable Shortening

1. Preheat oven to 350°F. Grease 13×9-inch baking pan. Place wire rack on countertop.

2. For Base, place brown sugar, peanut butter, shortening, milk and vanilla in large bowl. Beat at medium speed of electric mixer until well blended. Add egg; beat just until blended.

3. Combine flour, baking soda and salt in small bowl. Add to shortening mixture; beat at low speed just until blended.

4. Press mixture onto bottom of prepared pan.

5. Bake at 350°F for 18 to 20 minutes or until wooden pick inserted in center comes out clean. *Do not overbake.* Cool completely on wire rack.

6. For Peanut Butter Layer, place powdered sugar, peanut butter, shortening and milk in medium bowl. Beat at low speed of electric mixer until smooth. Spread over base. Refrigerate 30 minutes.

7. For Chocolate Glaze, place chocolate and shortening in small microwave-safe bowl. Microwave at 50% (MEDIUM) for 1 to 2 minutes or until shiny and soft. Stir until smooth. Cool slightly. Spread over peanut butter layer. Refrigerate about 1 hour or until glaze is set. Cut into 3×1½-inch bars. Let stand 15 to 20 minutes at room temperature before serving.

Makes about 2 dozen bars

Triple Layer Peanut Butter Bars

BROWNIES

DECADENT BLONDE BROWNIES

½ cup butter or margarine, softened
¾ cup granulated sugar
¾ cup firmly packed light brown sugar
2 large eggs
2 teaspoons vanilla
1½ cups all-purpose flour
1 teaspoon baking powder
½ teaspoon salt
1 package (10 ounces) semisweet chocolate chunks
1 jar (3½ ounces) macadamia nuts, coarsely chopped

Preheat oven to 350°F. Beat butter, granulated sugar and brown sugar in large bowl with electric mixer at medium speed until light and fluffy. Beat in eggs and vanilla. Add combined flour, baking powder and salt. Stir until well blended. Stir in chocolate chunks and macadamia nuts. Spread evenly into greased 13×9-inch baking pan. Bake 25 to 30 minutes or until golden brown. Remove pan to wire rack; cool completely. Cut into 3¼×1½-inch bars. *Makes about 2 dozen brownies*

BROWNIES

RASPBERRY FUDGE BROWNIES

½ cup butter or margarine
3 squares (1 ounce each) bittersweet
    chocolate*
2 eggs
1 cup sugar
1 teaspoon vanilla
¾ cup all-purpose flour
¼ teaspoon baking powder
    Dash salt
½ cup sliced or slivered almonds
½ cup raspberry preserves
1 cup (6 ounces) milk chocolate chips

*Bittersweet chocolate is available in specialty food stores. One square unsweetened chocolate plus 2 squares semisweet chocolate may be substituted.

Preheat oven to 350°F. Butter and flour 8-inch square baking pan. Melt butter and bittersweet chocolate in small, heavy saucepan over low heat. Remove from heat; cool. Beat eggs, sugar and vanilla in large bowl until light. Beat in chocolate mixture. Stir in flour, baking powder and salt until just blended. Spread ¾ of batter in prepared pan; sprinkle almonds over top. Bake 10 minutes. Remove from oven; spread preserves over almonds. Carefully spoon remaining batter over preserves, smoothing top. Bake 25 to 30 minutes or just until top feels firm. Remove from oven; sprinkle chocolate chips over top. Let stand a few minutes, then spread evenly over brownies. Cool completely. When chocolate is set, cut into squares.

Makes 16 brownies

WHITE CHOCOLATE CHUNK BROWNIES

4 squares (1 ounce each) unsweetened
    chocolate, coarsely chopped
½ cup butter or margarine
2 large eggs
1¼ cups granulated sugar
1 teaspoon vanilla
½ cup all-purpose flour
½ teaspoon salt
1 white baking bar (6 ounces), cut into
    ¼-inch pieces
½ cup coarsely chopped walnuts (optional)
    Powdered sugar for garnish

Preheat oven to 350°F. Melt unsweetened chocolate and butter in small, heavy saucepan over low heat, stirring constantly; set aside. Beat eggs in large bowl; gradually add granulated sugar, beating at medium speed about 4 minutes until very thick and lemon colored. Beat in chocolate mixture and vanilla. Beat in flour and salt just until blended. Stir in baking bar pieces and walnuts. Spread evenly into greased 8-inch square baking pan. Bake 30 minutes or until edges begin to pull away from sides of pan and center is set. Remove pan to wire rack; cool completely. Cut into 2-inch squares. Sprinkle with powdered sugar, if desired.

Makes about 16 brownies

Raspberry Fudge Brownies

BROWNIES

TOFFEE BROWNIE BARS

CRUST
  ¾ **cup butter or margarine, softened**
  ¾ **cup firmly packed brown sugar**
  1 **egg yolk**
  ¾ **teaspoon vanilla extract**
 1½ **cups all-purpose flour**

FILLING
  1 **package (19.8 ounces) DUNCAN HINES®**
    Fudge Brownie Mix
  1 **egg**
  ⅓ **cup water**
  ⅓ **cup CRISCO® Oil**

TOPPING
  1 **package (12 ounces) milk chocolate**
    chips, melted
  ¾ **cup finely chopped pecans**

1. Preheat oven to 350°F. Grease 15½×10½×1-inch jelly-roll pan.

2. For Crust, combine butter, brown sugar, egg yolk and vanilla extract in large bowl. Stir in flour. Spread in pan. Bake 15 minutes or until golden.

3. For Filling, combine brownie mix, egg, water and oil in large bowl. Stir with spoon until well blended, about 50 strokes. Spread over hot crust. Bake 15 minutes or until surface appears set. Cool 30 minutes.

4. For Topping, spread melted chocolate on top of brownie layer; garnish with pecans. Cool completely in pan on wire rack. Cut into bars.

Makes about 48 brownies

EXTRA MOIST & CHUNKY BROWNIES

  1 **(8-ounce) package cream cheese,**
    softened
  1 **cup sugar**
  1 **egg**
  1 **teaspoon vanilla extract**
  ¾ **cup all-purpose flour**
  1 **(4-serving size) package ROYAL®**
    Chocolate or Dark 'n' Sweet Chocolate
    Pudding & Pie Filling
  4 **(1-ounce) semisweet chocolate squares,**
    chopped

MICROWAVE DIRECTIONS: In large bowl, with electric mixer at high speed, beat cream cheese, sugar, egg and vanilla until smooth; blend in flour and pudding mix. Spread batter in greased 8×8×2-inch microwavable dish; sprinkle with chocolate. Microwave on HIGH (100% power) for 8 to 10 minutes or until toothpick inserted in center comes out clean, rotating dish ½ turn every 2 minutes. Cool completely in pan. Cut into squares. *Makes 16 squares*

Toffee Brownie Bars

BROWNIES

CARAMEL-LAYERED BROWNIES

- **4 squares BAKER'S® Unsweetened Chocolate**
- **¾ cup (1½ sticks) margarine or butter**
- **2 cups sugar**
- **3 eggs**
- **1 teaspoon vanilla**
- **1 cup all-purpose flour**
- **1 cup BAKER'S® Semi-Sweet Real Chocolate Chips**
- **1½ cups chopped nuts**
- **1 package (14 ounces) caramels**
- **⅓ cup evaporated milk**

HEAT oven to 350°F.

MICROWAVE chocolate and margarine in large microwavable bowl on HIGH 2 minutes or until margarine is melted. **Stir until chocolate is completely melted.**

STIR sugar into melted chocolate mixture. Mix in eggs and vanilla until well blended. Stir in flour. Remove 1 cup of batter; set aside. Spread remaining batter in greased 13×9-inch pan. Sprinkle with chips and 1 cup of the nuts.

MICROWAVE caramels and milk in same bowl on HIGH 4 minutes, stirring after 2 minutes. Stir until caramels are completely melted and smooth. Spoon over chips and nuts, spreading to edges of pan. Gently spread reserved batter over caramel mixture. Sprinkle with the remaining ½ cup nuts.

BAKE for 40 minutes or until toothpick inserted into center comes out with fudgy crumbs. **Do not overbake.** Cool in pan; cut into squares.

Makes about 24 brownies

BLONDE BRICKLE BROWNIES

- **1⅓ cups all-purpose flour**
- **½ teaspoon baking powder**
- **¼ teaspoon salt**
- **2 eggs**
- **½ cup granulated sugar**
- **½ cup firmly packed brown sugar**
- **⅓ cup butter or margarine, melted**
- **1 teaspoon vanilla**
- **¼ teaspoon almond extract**
- **1 package (6 ounces) BITS 'O BRICKLE®, divided**
- **½ cup chopped pecans (optional)**

Preheat oven to 350°F. Grease 8-inch square baking pan. Mix flour with baking powder and salt; set aside. In large bowl, beat eggs well. Gradually beat in granulated sugar and brown sugar until thick and creamy. Add butter, vanilla and almond extract; mix well. Gently stir in flour mixture until moistened. Fold in ⅔ cup Bits 'O Brickle® and nuts. Pour into prepared pan.

Bake 30 minutes. Remove from oven; immediately sprinkle remaining Bits 'O Brickle® over top. Cool completely in pan on wire rack. Cut into squares.

Makes about 16 brownies

Blonde Brickle Brownies

SCRUMPTIOUS MINTED BROWNIES

1 package (19.8 ounces) DUNCAN HINES®
   Fudge Brownie Mix
1 egg
⅓ cup water
⅓ cup CRISCO® Oil
48 chocolate crème de menthe candy wafers,
   divided

1. Preheat oven to 350°F. Grease bottom of 13×9×2-inch baking pan.

2. Combine brownie mix, egg, water and oil in large bowl. Stir with spoon until well blended, about 50 strokes. Spread in pan. Bake at 350°F for 25 minutes or until set. Place 30 candy wafers evenly over hot brownies. Let stand for 1 minute to melt. Spread candy wafers to frost brownies. Score frosting into 36 bars by running tip of knife through melted candy. (Do not cut through brownies.) Cut remaining 18 candy wafers in half lengthwise; place halves on each scored bar. Cool completely. Cut into bars.   *Makes 36 brownies*

TIP: For a unique garnish, in place of candy wafer halves, make chocolate mint wafer curls. Pull a vegetable peeler firmly across sides of candy wafers. Use long, thin strokes. Arrange on top of brownies while frosting is still soft.

BUFFALO BILL BROWNIES

1 (4-serving size) package ROYAL®
   Chocolate Pudding & Pie Filling
2 cups heavy cream
¼ cup raspberry preserves
1 prepared brownie mix in 9-inch square
   pan
¼ cup semisweet chocolate chips
1 tablespoon FLEISCHMANN'S® Margarine

In small saucepan, over medium heat, heat pudding, heavy cream and preserves to a boil; boil 1 minute. Pour pudding over prepared brownie; set aside.

In small saucepan, over medium heat, melt chocolate chips and margarine. Drizzle over pudding. Chill until firm, about 2 hours. Cut into 3-inch squares.   *Makes 9 servings*

Scrumptious Minted Brownies

BROWNIES

BROWNIE BON BONS

- 2 jars (10 ounces each) maraschino cherries with stems
- Cherry liqueur (optional)*
- 4 squares BAKER'S® Unsweetened Chocolate
- ¾ cup (1½ sticks) margarine or butter
- 2 cups granulated sugar
- 4 eggs
- 1 teaspoon vanilla
- 1 cup all-purpose flour
- Chocolate Fudge Filling (recipe follows)
- ½ cup powdered sugar

*For liqueur-flavored cherries, drain liquid from cherries. Do not remove cherries from jars. Refill jars with liqueur to completely cover cherries; cover tightly. Let stand at least 24 hours for best flavor.

HEAT oven to 350°F.

MICROWAVE chocolate and margarine in large microwavable bowl on HIGH 2 minutes or until margarine is melted. **Stir until chocolate is completely melted.**

STIR granulated sugar into melted chocolate mixture. Mix in eggs and vanilla until well blended. Stir in flour. Fill greased 1¾×1-inch miniature muffin cups ⅔ full with batter.

BAKE for 20 minutes or until toothpick inserted into center comes out with fudgy crumbs. **Do not overbake.** Cool slightly; loosen edges with tip of knife. Remove from pans. Turn each brownie onto wax paper-lined tray while warm. Make ½-inch indentation into top of each brownie with end of wooden spoon. Cool completely.

PREPARE Chocolate Fudge Filling. Drain cherries, reserving liquid or liqueur. Let cherries stand on paper towels to dry. Combine powdered sugar with enough reserved liquid to form a thin glaze.

SPOON or pipe about 1 teaspoon Chocolate Fudge Filling into indentation of each brownie. Gently press cherry into filling. Drizzle with powdered sugar glaze.   *Makes about 48 bon bons*

CHOCOLATE FUDGE FILLING
- 1 package (3 ounces) PHILADELPHIA BRAND® Cream Cheese, softened
- 1 teaspoon vanilla
- ¼ cup corn syrup
- 3 squares BAKER'S® Unsweetened Chocolate, melted and cooled
- 1 cup powdered sugar

BEAT cream cheese and vanilla in small bowl until smooth. Slowly pour in corn syrup, beating until well blended. Add chocolate; beat until smooth. Gradually add powdered sugar, beating until well blended and smooth.

Makes about 1 cup

Brownie Bon Bons

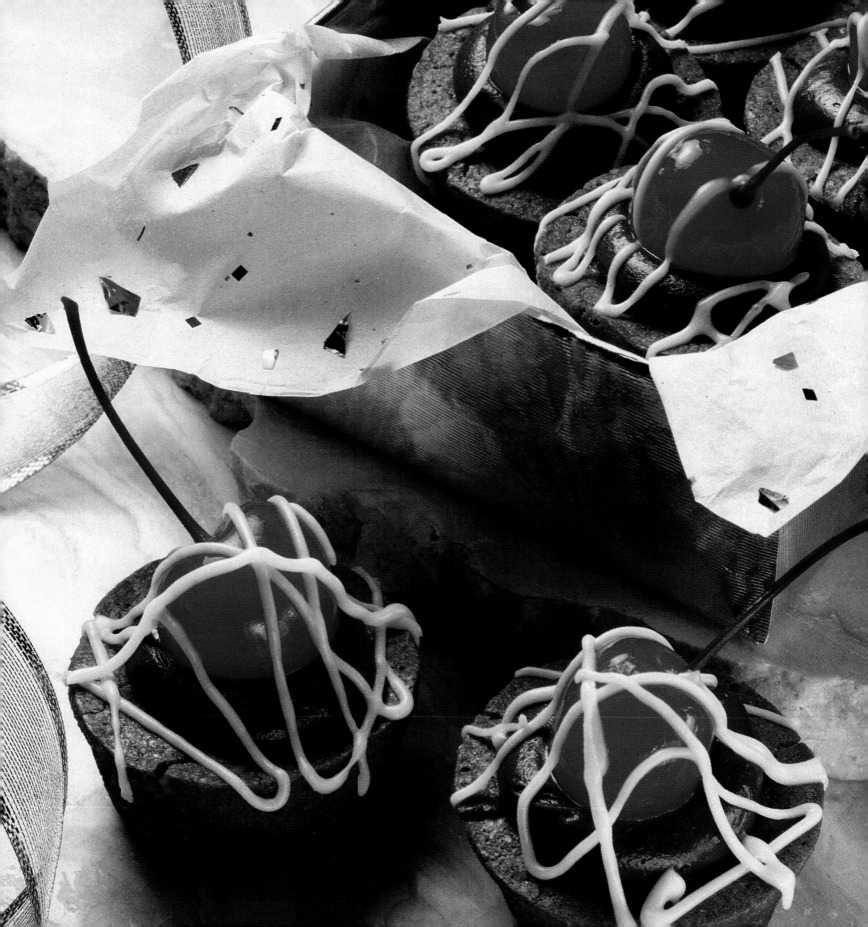

BROWNIES

COCONUT CROWNED CAPPUCCINO BROWNIES

6 squares (1 ounce each) semisweet chocolate, coarsely chopped
1 tablespoon freeze-dried coffee
1 tablespoon boiling water
¾ cup all-purpose flour
¾ teaspoon ground cinnamon
½ teaspoon baking powder
¼ teaspoon salt
½ cup sugar
¼ cup butter or margarine, softened
3 large eggs, divided
¼ cup whipping cream
1 teaspoon vanilla
¾ cup flaked coconut, divided
½ cup semisweet chocolate chips, divided

1. Preheat oven to 350°F. Grease 8-inch square baking pan; set aside.

2. Melt chocolate squares in small, heavy saucepan over low heat, stirring constantly; set aside. Dissolve coffee in boiling water in small cup; set aside.

3. In small bowl, combine flour, cinnamon, baking powder and salt.

4. Beat sugar and butter in large bowl with electric mixer at medium speed until light and fluffy. Beat in 2 eggs, 1 at a time, scraping down side of bowl after each addition. Beat in chocolate mixture and coffee mixture until well combined. Add flour mixture. Beat at low speed until well blended. Spread batter evenly into prepared pan.

5. For topping, combine cream, remaining 1 egg and vanilla in small bowl; mix well. Stir in ½ cup coconut and ¼ cup chips. Spread evenly over brownie base; sprinkle with remaining ¼ cup coconut and chips.

6. Bake 30 to 35 minutes or until coconut is browned and center is set. Remove pan to wire rack; cool completely. Cut into 2-inch squares. Store tightly covered at room temperature or freeze up to 3 months.   *Makes 16 brownies*

Coconut Crowned Cappuccino Brownies

BROWNIES

CHOCOLATEY ROCKY ROAD BROWNIES

BROWNIES

   1 cup butter or margarine
   4 squares (1 ounce each) unsweetened
      chocolate
1½ cups granulated sugar
   1 cup all-purpose flour
   3 eggs
1½ teaspoons vanilla
  ½ cup salted peanuts, chopped

FROSTING

  ¼ cup butter or margarine
   1 (3-ounce) package cream cheese
   1 square (1 ounce) unsweetened chocolate
  ¼ cup milk
2¾ cups powdered sugar
   1 teaspoon vanilla
   2 cups miniature marshmallows
   1 cup salted peanuts

For Brownies, preheat oven to 350°F. In 3-quart saucepan, combine 1 cup butter and 4 squares chocolate. Cook over medium heat, stirring constantly, until melted, 5 to 7 minutes. Add granulated sugar, flour, eggs and 1½ teaspoons vanilla; mix well. Stir in ½ cup chopped peanuts. Spread into greased 13×9-inch baking pan. Bake 20 to 25 minutes or until brownie starts to pull away from sides of pan. Cool completely.

For Frosting, in 2-quart saucepan, combine ¼ cup butter, cream cheese, 1 square chocolate and milk. Cook over medium heat, stirring occasionally, until melted, 6 to 8 minutes. Remove from heat; add powdered sugar and 1 teaspoon vanilla; beat with hand mixer until smooth. Stir in marshmallows and 1 cup peanuts. Immediately spread over cooled brownies. Cool completely; cut into bars. Store in refrigerator.   *Makes about 4 dozen brownies*

Chocolatey Rocky Road Brownies

— *Grandkids'* —

DELIGHTS

CHOCOLATE CHIP LOLLIPOPS

**1 package DUNCAN HINES® Chocolate Chip
Cookie Mix
1 egg
⅓ cup CRISCO® Oil
2 tablespoons water
Flat ice cream sticks
Assorted decors**

1. Preheat oven to 375°F.

2. Combine cookie mix, egg, oil and water in large bowl. Stir until thoroughly blended. Shape dough into 32 (1-inch) balls. Place balls 3 inches apart on ungreased cookie sheets. Push ice cream stick into center of each ball. Flatten dough ball with hand to form round lollipop. Decorate by pressing decors onto dough. Bake at 375°F for 8 to 9 minutes or until light golden brown. Cool 1 minute on cookie sheets. Remove to wire racks. Cool completely. Store in airtight container.

Makes 2½ to 3 dozen cookies

DELIGHTS

PEANUT BUTTER BEARS

1 cup **SKIPPY®** Creamy Peanut Butter
1 cup **MAZOLA®** Margarine, softened
1 cup firmly packed brown sugar
⅔ cup **KARO®** Light or Dark Corn Syrup
2 eggs
4 cups all-purpose flour, divided
1 tablespoon baking powder
1 teaspoon ground cinnamon (optional)
¼ teaspoon salt

In large bowl, with mixer at medium speed, beat peanut butter, margarine, brown sugar, corn syrup and eggs until smooth. Reduce speed; beat in 2 cups of the flour, the baking powder, cinnamon and salt. With spoon, stir in remaining 2 cups flour. Wrap dough in plastic wrap; refrigerate 2 hours.

Preheat oven to 325°F. Divide dough in half; set aside half. On floured surface, roll out half the dough to ⅛-inch thickness. Cut with floured bear cookie cutter. Repeat with remaining dough. Bake on ungreased cookie sheets 10 minutes or until lightly browned. Remove from cookie sheets; cool completely on wire rack. Decorate as desired.

Makes about 3 dozen bears

Prep Time: 35 minutes, plus chilling
Bake Time: 10 minutes, plus cooling

NOTE: Use scraps of dough to make bear faces. Make one small ball of dough for muzzle. Form 3 smaller balls of dough and press gently to create eyes and nose; bake as directed. If desired, use frosting to create paws, ears and bow ties.

MARSHMALLOW KRISPIE BARS

1 package (19.8 ounces) **DUNCAN HINES®** Fudge Brownie Mix
1 package (10½ ounces) miniature marshmallows
1½ cups semi-sweet chocolate chips
1 cup **JIF®** Creamy Peanut Butter
1 tablespoon butter or margarine
1½ cups crisp rice cereal

1. Preheat oven to 350°F. Grease bottom of 13×9×2-inch baking pan.

2. Prepare and bake brownies following package directions for original recipe. Remove from oven. Sprinkle marshmallows on hot brownies. Return to oven. Bake for 3 minutes longer.

3. Place chocolate chips, peanut butter and butter in medium saucepan. Cook on low heat, stirring constantly, until chips are melted. Add rice cereal; mix well. Spread mixture over marshmallow layer. Refrigerate until chilled. Cut into bars.

Makes 24 bars

Peanut Butter Bears

DELIGHTS

PEANUT BUTTER PIZZA COOKIES

1 package DUNCAN HINES® Peanut Butter Cookie Mix
1 egg
¼ cup CRISCO® Oil
1 tablespoon water
Sugar
1 container (16 ounces) DUNCAN HINES® Creamy Homestyle Chocolate Frosting
Cashews
Candy-coated chocolate pieces
Gumdrops, halved
Flaked coconut
½ bar (2 ounces) white chocolate baking bar
1½ teaspoons CRISCO® All-Vegetable Shortening

1. Preheat oven to 375°F.

2. Combine cookie mix, peanut butter packet from Mix, egg, oil and water in large bowl. Stir until thoroughly blended. Shape into 12 (2-inch) balls (about 3 level tablespoons each). Place balls 3½ inches apart on ungreased cookie sheets. Flatten with bottom of large glass dipped in sugar to make 3-inch circles. Bake at 375°F for 9 to 11 minutes or until set. Cool 1 minute on cookie sheets. Remove to wire racks. Cool completely.

3. Frost cookies with Chocolate frosting. Decorate with cashews, candy pieces, gumdrops and coconut. Melt white chocolate and shortening in small saucepan on low heat, stirring constantly, until smooth. Drizzle over cookies.

Makes 12 large cookies

CRUMBLE BARS

½ cup butter or margarine
1 cup all-purpose flour
¾ cup quick-cooking oats, uncooked
⅓ cup firmly packed light brown sugar
½ teaspoon salt
½ teaspoon baking soda
½ teaspoon vanilla extract
4 MILKY WAY® Bars (2.15 ounces each), each cut into 8 slices

Preheat oven to 350°F. Lightly grease 8×8×2-inch baking pan; set aside.

Melt butter in large saucepan. Remove from heat; stir in flour, oats, sugar, salt, baking soda and vanilla. Blend until crumbly. Press ⅔ of mixture into prepared pan. Arrange MILKY WAY® Bar slices in pan to within ½ inch from edges. Finely crumble remaining mixture over the MILKY WAY® Bars. Bake 20 to 25 minutes or until edges are golden brown. Cool in pan on wire rack. Cut into bars or squares to serve.

Makes 12 to 16 bars

Peanut Butter Pizza Cookies

DELIGHTS

WATERMELON SLICES

- **1 package DUNCAN HINES® Golden Sugar Cookie Mix**
- **1 egg**
- **¼ cup CRISCO® Oil**
- **1½ tablespoons water**
- **12 drops red food coloring**
- **5 drops green food coloring**
- **Chocolate sprinkles**

1. Combine cookie mix, egg, oil and water in large bowl. Stir until thoroughly blended; reserve ⅓ cup dough.

2. For red cookie dough, combine remaining dough with red food coloring. Stir until evenly tinted. On waxed paper, shape dough into 12-inch-long roll with one side flattened. Cover; refrigerate with flat side down until firm.

3. For green cookie dough, combine reserved ⅓ cup dough with green food coloring in small bowl. Stir until evenly tinted. Place between 2 layers of waxed paper. Roll dough into 12×4-inch rectangle. Refrigerate for 15 minutes.

4. Preheat oven to 375°F.

5. To assemble, remove green dough rectangle from refrigerator. Remove top layer of waxed paper. Trim edges along both 12-inch sides. Remove red dough log from refrigerator. Place red dough log, flattened side up, along center of green dough. Mold green dough up to edge of flattened side of red dough. Remove bottom layer of waxed paper. Trim excess green dough, if necessary.

6. Cut chilled roll with flat side down into ¼-inch-thick slices with sharp knife. Place 2 inches apart on ungreased cookie sheets. Sprinkle chocolate sprinkles on red dough for seeds. Bake at 375°F for 7 minutes or until set. Cool 1 minute on cookie sheets. Remove to wire racks. Cool completely. Store between layers of waxed paper in airtight container.   *Makes 3 to 4 dozen cookies*

TIP: To make neat, clean slices, use unwaxed dental floss.

Watermelon Slices

PEANUT BUTTER REINDEER

COOKIES:
  1 package DUNCAN HINES® Peanut Butter Cookie Mix
  1 egg
  ¼ cup CRISCO® Oil
  4 teaspoons all-purpose flour, divided

ASSORTED DECORATIONS:
  Miniature semi-sweet chocolate chips
  Vanilla milk chips
  Candy-coated semi-sweet chocolate chips
  Colored sprinkles

1. For Cookies, combine cookie mix, peanut butter packet from Mix, egg and oil in large bowl. Stir until thoroughly blended. Form dough into ball; divide in half to make 2 balls. Place 2 teaspoons of flour in gallon size (10⁹⁄₁₆×11-inch) resealable plastic bag. Place one ball of dough in bag. Seal bag; shake to coat with flour. Place dough in center of bag; unseal. Roll dough with rolling pin out to edges of bag. Slide bag onto baking sheet. Repeat with remaining 2 teaspoons flour, second plastic bag and remaining dough ball. Chill in refrigerator at least 1 hour.

2. Preheat oven to 375°F.

3. Use scissors to cut one bag down center and across ends. Turn plastic back to uncover dough. Dip reindeer cookie cutter in flour. Cut dough with reindeer cookie cutter. Dip cookie cutter in flour after each cut. Transfer cutout cookie to ungreased cookie sheets using a pancake turner. Decorate as desired making eyes, mouth, nose and tail with assorted decorations. Bake at 375°F for 5 to 7 minutes or until set but not browned. Cool 2 minutes on cookie sheet. Remove to wire racks. Cool completely. Repeat with remaining chilled dough. Store cookies between layers of waxed paper in airtight container.

Makes about 2 dozen cookies

TIPS: Reroll dough by folding plastic back over dough. To use as ornaments, press end of drinking straw in top of each unbaked cookie to make hole. Press straw through cookie again after baking. String ribbon through holes of cooled cookies. Tie at top.

Peanut Butter Reindeer

WALNUT CHRISTMAS BALLS

  1 cup California walnuts
  ⅔ cup powdered sugar, divided
  1 cup butter or margarine, softened
  1 teaspoon vanilla
1¾ cups all-purpose flour
    Chocolate Filling (recipe follows)

Preheat oven to 350°F. In food processor or blender, process walnuts with 2 tablespoons sugar until finely ground. In large bowl, cream butter and remaining sugar. Beat in vanilla. Add flour and ¾ cup walnut mixture; beat until blended. Roll dough into about 3 dozen walnut-size balls. Place 2 inches apart on ungreased cookie sheets.

Bake 10 to 12 minutes or until just golden around edges. Remove to wire racks to cool completely. Prepare Chocolate Filling. Place generous teaspoonful of filling on flat side of half the cookies. Top with remaining cookies, flat side down, forming sandwiches. Roll chocolate edges of cookies in remaining ground walnuts.

Makes about 1½ dozen sandwich cookies

CHOCOLATE FILLING: Chop 3 squares (1 ounce each) semisweet chocolate into small pieces; place in food processor or blender with ½ teaspoon vanilla. In small saucepan, heat 2 tablespoons *each* butter or margarine and whipping cream over medium heat until hot; pour over chocolate. Process until chocolate is melted, turning machine off and scraping sides as needed. With machine running, gradually add 1 cup powdered sugar; process until smooth.

*Favorite recipe from **Walnut Marketing Board***

BANANA CRESCENTS

½ cup DOLE® Chopped Almonds, toasted
  6 tablespoons sugar, divided
½ cup margarine, cut into pieces
1½ cups plus 2 tablespoons all-purpose flour
⅛ teaspoon salt
  1 extra-ripe, medium DOLE® Banana, peeled
  2 to 3 ounces semisweet chocolate chips

Pulverize almonds with 2 tablespoons sugar in food processor.

Beat margarine, almond mixture, remaining 4 tablespoons sugar, flour and salt.

Puree banana; add to batter and mix until well blended.

Using 1 tablespoon batter, roll into log then shape into crescent. Place on ungreased cookie sheet. Bake in 375°F oven 25 minutes or until golden. Cool on wire rack.

Melt chocolate in microwavable dish at 50% power 1½ to 2 minutes, stirring once. Dip ends of cookies in chocolate. Refrigerate until chocolate hardens.

Makes 2 dozen cookies

Banana Crescents

GLAZED SUGAR COOKIES

COOKIES
   1 package **DUNCAN HINES®** Golden Sugar
      Cookie Mix
   1 egg
   ¼ cup **CRISCO®** Oil
   1 teaspoon water

GLAZE
  1½ cups sifted powdered sugar
   2 to 3 tablespoons water or milk
   ¾ teaspoons vanilla extract
     Food coloring
     Red and green sugar crystals, nonpareils
      or cinnamon candies

1. Preheat oven to 375°F.

2. For Cookies, combine cookie mix, egg, oil and water in large bowl. Stir thoroughly until blended. Roll dough to ¼-inch thickness on lightly floured surface. Cut dough into desired shapes using floured cookie cutters. Place cookies 2 inches apart on ungreased cookie sheets. Bake at 375°F for 7 to 8 minutes or until edges are light golden brown. Cool 1 minute on cookie sheets. Remove to wire racks. Cool completely.

3. For Glaze, combine powdered sugar, water and vanilla extract in medium bowl. Beat until smooth. Tint glaze with food coloring, if desired. Brush glaze on each cookie with a clean pastry brush. Sprinkle each cookie with sugar crystals, nonpareils or cinnamon candies before glaze sets. Allow glaze to set before storing between layers of waxed paper in air-tight container.

Makes 4 dozen cookies

TIP: Use Duncan Hines Creamy Homestyle Vanilla Frosting for a quick glaze. Heat frosting in opened container in microwave oven at HIGH (100% power) for 10 to 15 seconds. Stir well. Spread on cookies and decorate as desired before frosting sets.

Glazed Sugar Cookies

DANISH RASPBERRY RIBBONS

COOKIES
   1 cup butter, softened
   ½ cup granulated sugar
   1 large egg
   2 tablespoons milk
   2 tablespoons vanilla
   ¼ teaspoon almond extract
   2 to 2⅔ cups all-purpose flour, divided
   6 tablespoons seedless raspberry jam

GLAZE
   ½ cup sifted powdered sugar
   1 tablespoon milk
   1 teaspoon vanilla

1. For Cookies, beat butter and granulated sugar in bowl with mixer at medium speed until fluffy. Beat in egg, 2 tablespoons milk, 2 tablespoons vanilla and almond extract until blended.

2. Gradually add 1½ cups flour. Beat at low speed until well blended. Stir in additional flour with spoon until stiff dough forms. Wrap in plastic wrap and refrigerate until firm, 30 minutes or overnight.

3. Preheat oven to 375°F. Cut dough into 6 pieces. Rewrap 3 pieces; refrigerate. With floured hands, shape each dough piece into 12-inch-long, ¾-inch-thick rope.

4. Place ropes 2 inches apart on *ungreased* cookie sheets. Make a ¼-inch-deep groove down center of each rope with handle of wooden spoon. (Ropes flatten to ½-inch-thick strips.)

5. Bake 12 minutes. Spoon 1 tablespoon jam along each groove. Bake 5 to 7 minutes longer or until strips are light golden brown. Cool strips 15 minutes on cookie sheets.

6. For Glaze, place powdered sugar, 1 tablespoon milk and 1 teaspoon vanilla in small bowl; stir until smooth. Drizzle Glaze over strips; let stand 5 minutes to dry. Cut strips at 45° angle into 1-inch slices. Cool cookies completely on wire racks. Repeat with remaining dough. Store tightly covered between sheets of waxed paper at room temperature. *Makes about 5½ dozen cookies*

Danish Raspberry Ribbons

PEANUT BUTTER CUT-OUTS

½ cup SKIPPY® Creamy Peanut Butter
6 tablespoons MAZOLA® Margarine or
butter, softened
½ cup firmly packed brown sugar
⅓ cup KARO® Light or Dark Corn Syrup
1 egg
2 cups all-purpose flour, divided
1½ teaspoons baking powder
1 teaspoon ground cinnamon (optional)
⅛ teaspoon salt

In large bowl, with mixer at medium speed, beat peanut butter, margarine, brown sugar, corn syrup and egg until smooth. Reduce speed; beat in 1 cup flour, baking powder, cinnamon and salt. With spoon, stir in remaining 1 cup flour.

Divide dough in half. Between two sheets of waxed paper on large cookie sheets, roll each half of dough to ¼-inch thickness. Refrigerate until firm, about 1 hour.

Preheat oven to 350°F. Remove top piece of waxed paper. With floured cookie cutters, cut dough into shapes. Place on ungreased cookie sheets. Bake 10 minutes or until lightly browned. *Do not overbake.* Let stand on cookie sheets 2 minutes. Remove from cookie sheets; cool completely on wire racks. Reroll dough trimmings and cut. Decorate as desired. *Makes about 5 dozen cookies*

NOTE: Use scraps of dough to create details on cookies.

BAVARIAN COOKIE WREATHS

3½ cups unsifted all-purpose flour
1 cup sugar, divided
3 teaspoons grated orange peel, divided
¼ teaspoon salt
1⅓ cups butter or margarine
¼ cup Florida orange juice
⅓ cup finely chopped blanched almonds
1 egg white beaten with 1 teaspoon water
Prepared frosting (optional)

Preheat oven to 400°F. In large bowl, mix flour, ¾ cup sugar, 2 teaspoons orange peel and salt. Using pastry blender, cut in butter and orange juice until mixture holds together. Knead few times and press into a ball.

Shape dough into ¾-inch balls; lightly roll each ball on floured board into a 6-inch-long strip. Using two strips, twist together to make a rope. Pinch ends of rope together to make a wreath; place on lightly greased baking sheet.

In shallow dish, mix almonds, remaining ¼ cup sugar and 1 teaspoon orange peel. Brush top of each wreath with egg white mixture and sprinkle with sugar-almond mixture.

Bake 8 to 10 minutes or until lightly browned. Remove to wire racks; cool completely. Frost, if desired. *Makes 5 dozen cookies*

Favorite recipe from **Florida Department of Citrus**

Peanut Butter Cut-Outs

PECAN DATE BARS

CRUST
⅓ cup butter or margarine
1 package DUNCAN HINES® Moist Deluxe
    White Cake Mix
1 egg

TOPPING
1 (8-ounce) package chopped dates
1¼ cups chopped pecans
1 cup water
½ teaspoon vanilla extract
Powdered sugar

1. Preheat oven to 350°F. Grease and flour 13×9-inch pan.

2. For Crust, cut butter into cake mix with a pastry blender or 2 knives until mixture is crumbly. Add egg; stir well (mixture will be crumbly). Press mixture into bottom of prepared pan.

3. For Topping, combine dates, pecans and water in medium saucepan. Bring to a boil. Reduce heat and simmer until mixture thickens, stirring constantly. Remove from heat. Stir in vanilla extract. Spread date mixture evenly over crust. Bake 25 to 30 minutes. Cool completely. Dust with powdered sugar.   *Makes about 32 bars*

BLACK RUSSIAN BROWNIES

4 squares (1 ounce each) unsweetened
    chocolate
1 cup butter
¾ teaspoon black pepper
4 eggs, lightly beaten
1½ cups sugar
1½ teaspoons vanilla
⅓ cup KAHLÚA®
2 tablespoons vodka
1⅓ cups all-purpose flour
½ teaspoon salt
¼ teaspoon baking powder
1 cup chopped walnuts or toasted sliced
    almonds
Powdered sugar (optional)

Line bottom of 13×9-inch baking pan with waxed paper. Melt chocolate and butter with pepper in small saucepan over low heat. Remove from heat.

Combine eggs, sugar and vanilla in large bowl; beat well. Stir in cooled chocolate mixture, Kahlúa and vodka. Combine flour, salt and baking powder; add to chocolate mixture and stir until blended. Add walnuts. Spread in prepared pan.

Bake in 350°F oven just until toothpick inserted into center comes out clean, about 25 minutes. *Do not overbake.* Cool in pan on wire rack. Cut into bars. Sprinkle with powdered sugar, if desired.
          Makes about 30 brownies

Pecan Date Bars

GERMAN HONEY BARS

2¾ cups all-purpose flour
2 teaspoons ground cinnamon
1 teaspoon baking powder
½ teaspoon baking soda
½ teaspoon salt
½ teaspoon ground cardamom
½ teaspoon ground ginger
½ cup honey
½ cup dark molasses
¾ cup firmly packed brown sugar
3 tablespoons butter, melted
1 large egg
½ cup chopped toasted almonds (optional)
Glaze (recipe follows)

1. Preheat oven to 350°F. Grease 15×10-inch jelly-roll pan; set aside.

2. Combine flour, cinnamon, baking powder, baking soda, salt, cardamom and ginger in medium bowl.

3. Combine honey and molasses in medium saucepan; bring to a boil over medium heat. Remove from heat; cool 10 minutes.

4. Stir brown sugar, butter and egg into honey mixture.

5. Place brown sugar mixture in large bowl. Gradually add flour mixture. Beat at low speed with electric mixer until dough forms. Stir in almonds with spoon. (Dough will be slightly sticky.)

6. Spread dough evenly into prepared pan. Bake 20 to 22 minutes or until golden brown and set. Remove pan to wire rack; cool completely.

7. Prepare Glaze. Spread over cooled cookie base. Let stand until set, about 30 minutes. Cut into 2×1-inch bars. Store tightly covered at room temperature or freeze up to 3 months.

Makes about 6 dozen bars

GLAZE
1¼ cups sifted powdered sugar
3 tablespoons fresh lemon juice
1 teaspoon grated lemon peel

Place all ingredients in medium bowl; stir with spoon until smooth.

German Honey Bars

LINZER SANDWICH COOKIES

1⅓ cups all-purpose flour
¼ teaspoon baking powder
¼ teaspoon salt
¾ cup sugar
½ cup butter, softened
1 large egg
1 teaspoon vanilla
   Seedless raspberry jam

1. Combine flour, baking powder and salt in small bowl.

2. Beat sugar and butter in medium bowl with electric mixer at medium speed until light and fluffy. Beat in egg and vanilla. Gradually add flour mixture. Beat at low speed until dough forms.

3. Form dough into 2 discs; wrap in plastic wrap and refrigerate 2 hours or until firm.

4. Preheat oven to 375°F. Working with 1 disc at a time, unwrap dough and place on lightly floured surface. Roll out dough with lightly floured rolling pin.

5. Cut dough into desired shapes with floured cookie cutters. Cut out equal numbers of each shape. (If dough becomes soft, cover and refrigerate several minutes before continuing.)

6. Cut 1-inch centers out of half the cookies of each shape. Gently press dough trimmings together; reroll and cut out more cookies. Place cookies 1½ to 2 inches apart on *ungreased* cookie sheets.

7. Bake 7 to 9 minutes or until edges are lightly browned. Let cookies stand on cookie sheet 1 to 2 minutes. Remove cookies with spatula to wire racks; cool completely. To assemble cookies, spread 1 teaspoon jam on flat side of whole cookies, spreading almost to edges. Place cookies with holes, flat-side down, on jam. Store tightly covered at room temperature or freeze up to 3 months.

Makes about 2 dozen cookies

WALNUT–BRANDY SHORTBREAD

1 cup butter
½ cup firmly packed brown sugar
⅛ teaspoon salt
2 tablespoons brandy
1 cup all-purpose flour
1 cup finely chopped toasted California
   walnuts
   Granulated sugar

Cream butter with brown sugar and salt in large bowl; mix in brandy. Gradually add flour; stir in walnuts. Spread in ungreased 9-inch square pan. Refrigerate 30 minutes.

Pierce mixture all over with fork. Bake at 325°F about 55 minutes or until dark golden brown. If dough puffs up during baking, pierce again with fork. Sprinkle lightly with granulated sugar and cool. Cut into squares with sharp knife.

Makes 36 squares

Favorite recipe from **Walnut Marketing Board**

Linzer Sandwich Cookies

Acknowledgments

The publishers would like to thank the companies and organizations listed below for the use of their recipes and photos in this publication.

Best Foods, a Division of CPC International Inc.

California Apricot Advisory Board

Dole Food Company, Inc.

Florida Department of Citrus

Hershey Foods Corporation

Kahlúa Liqueur

Kraft Foods, Inc.

Leaf®, Inc.

M&M/Mars

Nabisco, Inc.

Nestlé Food Company

The Procter & Gamble Company

The Quaker Oats Company

Ralston Foods, Inc.

Sunkist Growers

Walnut Marketing Board

—Index—

METRIC CONVERSION CHART

VOLUME MEASUREMENTS (dry)

1/8 teaspoon = 0.5 mL
1/4 teaspoon = 1 mL
1/2 teaspoon = 2 mL
3/4 teaspoon = 4 mL
1 teaspoon = 5 mL
1 tablespoon = 15 mL
2 tablespoons = 30 mL
1/4 cup = 60 mL
1/3 cup = 75 mL
1/2 cup = 125 mL
2/3 cup = 150 mL
3/4 cup = 175 mL
1 cup = 250 mL
2 cups = 1 pint = 500 mL
3 cups = 750 mL
4 cups = 1 quart = 1 L

VOLUME MEASUREMENTS (fluid)

1 fluid ounce (2 tablespoons) = 30 mL
4 fluid ounces (1/2 cup) = 125 mL
8 fluid ounces (1 cup) = 250 mL
12 fluid ounces (1 1/2 cups) = 375 mL
16 fluid ounces (2 cups) = 500 mL

WEIGHTS (mass)

1/2 ounce = 15 g
1 ounce = 30 g
3 ounces = 90 g
4 ounces = 120 g
8 ounces = 225 g
10 ounces = 285 g
12 ounces = 360 g
16 ounces = 1 pound = 450 g

DIMENSIONS

1/16 inch = 2 mm
1/8 inch = 3 mm
1/4 inch = 6 mm
1/2 inch = 1.5 cm
3/4 inch = 2 cm
1 inch = 2.5 cm

OVEN TEMPERATURES

250°F = 120°C
275°F = 140°C
300°F = 150°C
325°F = 160°C
350°F = 180°C
375°F = 190°C
400°F = 200°C
425°F = 220°C
450°F = 230°C

BAKING PAN SIZES

Utensil	Size in Inches/Quarts	Metric Volume	Size in Centimeters
Baking or	8 × 8 × 2	2 L	20 × 20 × 5
Cake Pan	9 × 9 × 2	2.5 L	22 × 22 × 5
(square or	12 × 8 × 2	3 L	30 × 20 × 5
rectangular)	13 × 9 × 2	3.5 L	33 × 23 × 5
Loaf Pan	8 × 4 × 3	1.5 L	20 × 10 × 7
	9 × 5 × 3	2 L	23 × 13 × 7
Round Layer	8 × 1½	1.2 L	20 × 4
Cake Pan	9 × 1½	1.5 L	23 × 4
Pie Plate	8 × 1¼	750 mL	20 × 3
	9 × 1¼	1 L	23 × 3
Baking Dish	1 quart	1 L	—
or Casserole	1½ quart	1.5 L	—
	2 quart	2 L	—